Coral Reefs

by Margie O'Hern

Scott Foresman
is an imprint of

Glenview, Illinois • Boston, Massachusetts • Chandler, Arizona •
Upper Saddle River, New Jersey

Photographs

Every effort has been made to secure permission and provide appropriate credit for photographic material. The publisher deeply regrets any omission and pledges to correct errors called to its attention in subsequent editions.

Unless otherwise acknowledged, all photographs are the property of Pearson Education, Inc.

Photo locators denoted as follows: Top (T), Center (C), Bottom (B), Left (L), Right (R), Background (Bkgd)

Opener Poelzer Wolfgang/Alamy Images; **1** Poelzer Wolfgang/Alamy Images; **3** Darryl Leniuk/Masterfile Corporation; **4** Imagebroker/Alamy Images; **5** Visual&Written SL/Alamy Images; **6** Jose B. Ruiz/Alamy Images; **7** Luciano Corbella/©DK Images; **8** NASA, Suzanne Long/Alamy Images; **9** Gerald Nowak/Getty Images; **10** ©DK Images; **11** Poelzer Wolfgang/Alamy Images; **12** ©David Peart/©DK Images; **13** Jeff Hunter/Getty Images; **14** Peter Scoones/Nature Picture Library; **15** Andre Seale/Alamy Images; **16** ©Jurgen Freund/Nature Picture Library; **17** Peter Scoones/Nature Picture Library; **18** Mark Conlin/Alamy Images; **19** Bojan Brecelj/Corbis; **20** ©Image Source; **21** ©David Peart/©DK Images; **22** Timothy O'Keefe/Alamy Images.

ISBN 13: 978-0-328-51397-0
ISBN 10:   0-328-51397-0

11 12 13 V0FL 17 16 15 14

What Is a Coral Reef?

Welcome to the undersea world of the **coral reef**. A coral reef is a ridge of hard rock in the ocean. Thousands of different plants and animals live on coral reefs. Coral reefs need sunlight. They are found in shallow water so that sunlight can reach the plants that grow on the reef. Coral reefs need warm, salty water. They are found in the ocean in the warmest parts of the world.

Coral reefs are formed by millions of tiny animals called corals. It takes a long time for coral reefs to form. Most coral reefs are 5,000 to 10,000 years old. Some may be as old as 245 million years.

Coral reef

3

Different Types of Corals

Coral reefs contain two types of corals: hard corals and soft corals. Hard corals are tiny animals that create their own hard outer skeleton. Many of these tiny skeletons are connected to create a colony. A **colony** is a group of animals living close together. When the corals die, the skeletons become part of the reef.

One example of hard coral is brain coral. It's called brain coral because it looks like the human brain. Many tiny coral animals, connected by their skeletons, form the brain coral.

Brain coral

Cladiella soft coral

Soft corals look like plants, but they are animals. They do not create a hard outer skeleton as the hard corals do. That's why they are called soft corals. Soft corals do not help build the coral reefs. Soft corals do not need as much sunlight as hard corals. They can live in deeper water than hard corals.

Coral Polyps

An individual coral is called a polyp. A **coral polyp** is a tiny ocean animal that is about the size of your thumbnail. Its body is shaped like a tube. At the top of the polyp is a mouth. Around the mouth are tiny armlike parts called **tentacles**. Tentacles have stingers that are used for catching food. A coral polyp has a soft body and a hard outer skeleton. The polyp usually rests on its cup-shaped skeleton, but it can go inside the skeleton to protect itself.

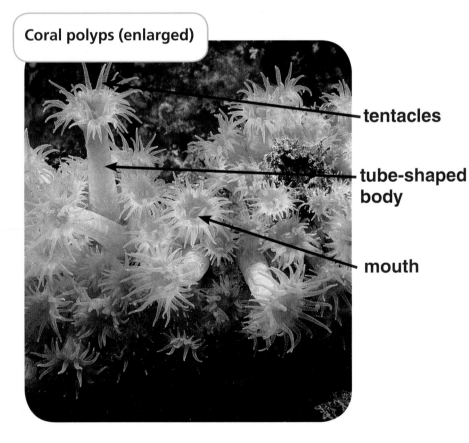

Coral polyps (enlarged)

tentacles

tube-shaped body

mouth

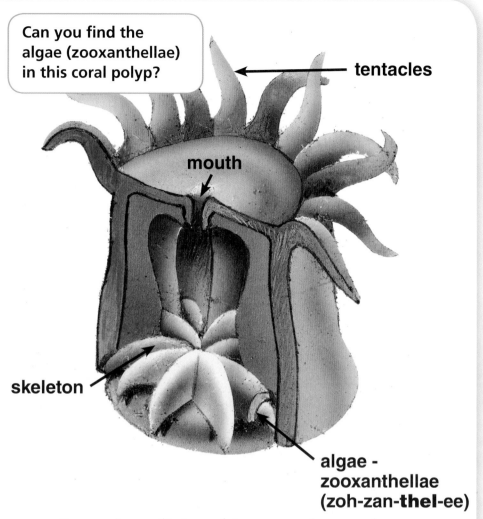

Can you find the algae (zooxanthellae) in this coral polyp?

tentacles

mouth

skeleton

algae - zooxanthellae (zoh-zan-**thel**-ee)

Sometimes living things work together and help each other. **Algae** are very simple living things. They grow in water. On a coral reef, coral polyps work with a very tiny kind of algae. These algae and the coral polyps help each other. Many of these tiny algae live inside each coral polyp. The algae make food for the coral polyp. The coral polyp protects the algae and helps them in other ways.

Different Kinds of Coral Reefs

There are three major kinds of coral reefs: fringing reefs, barrier reefs, and **atolls**. Fringing reefs are very young. They form very close to a mainland or island. There is not much water between the reef and the shore.

A barrier reef is separated from a mainland or island shore by a deep **lagoon**. A lagoon is a body of salt water that is separated from the ocean by the reef.

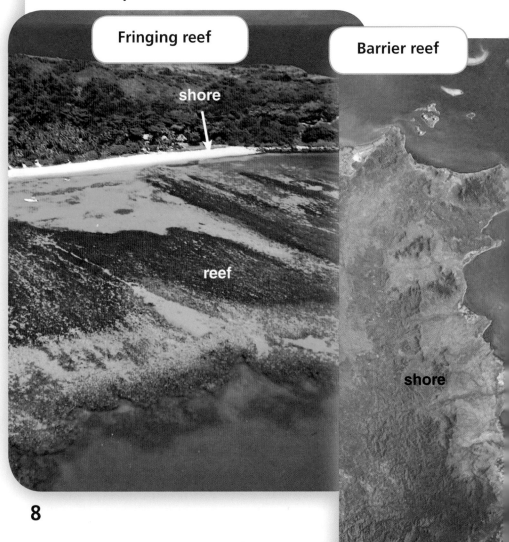

Fringing reef

shore

reef

Barrier reef

shore

An atoll is a circular reef that goes around a lagoon. Most atolls start as fringing reefs around an island. Over millions of years, the island sinks in the ocean and the reefs remain. Often, part of the island remains above water too.

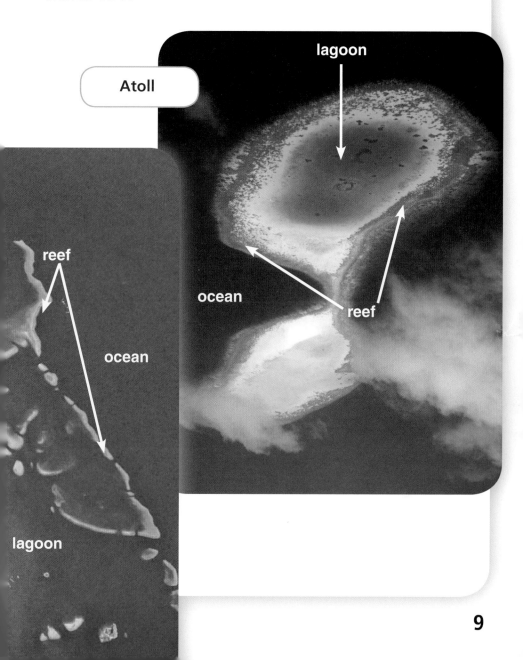

Atoll

lagoon

reef

ocean

ocean

reef

lagoon

Where Are Coral Reefs?

Most coral reefs are found in the tropics. Look at the map on this page. You can see that the tropics are near the equator in the warmest part of the world. The ocean water in the tropics is 68°F–82°F (20°C–28°C).

There are many coral reefs in the Pacific Ocean and the Indian Ocean. The Atlantic Ocean has fewer reefs because the water is colder. In the United States, only Florida and Hawaii have warm enough water to have coral reefs.

Locations of coral reefs are in red.

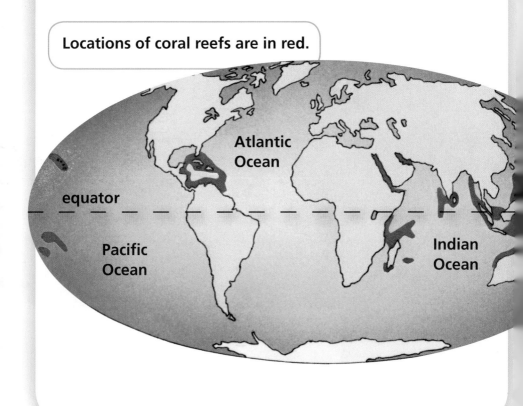

Atlantic
Ocean

equator

Pacific
Ocean

Indian
Ocean

Why Are Coral Reefs Important?

Coral reefs are important for many reasons. They protect the nearby land from strong waves and storms. Coral reefs provide food and a home for many plants and animals. More than 25 percent of ocean animals live in coral reefs, which are only a small part of the ocean.

Coral reefs provide food for many people in the world. Tourists enjoy the beauty of the coral reefs. In addition, coral reefs are a source of medicine to help sick people. People who live near the reefs earn money by fishing. Others make money serving the tourists.

Animals on Coral Reefs

The Great Barrier Reef is the largest coral reef in the world. It runs along the northeastern coast of Australia for 1,400 miles. More than 7,000 different kinds of animals live on this reef. The dugongs and the sea turtles are just two of those kinds of animals.

Large numbers of dugongs live on the Great Barrier Reef. Dugongs are sometimes called sea cows. They grow to be more than nine feet long. They weigh more than 800 pounds and live to be 70 years old.

Dugong

Sea turtle

Six different kinds of sea turtles live on the Great Barrier Reef. Sea turtles leave the water to lay their eggs. They use their flippers to move along the sandy beach. Then they dig a hole with their flippers and lay their eggs in the hole. They lay up to 100 eggs at one time. They fill up the hole with sand to cover their eggs. When the baby turtles are born, they ride the ocean waves back to the water. The largest sea turtle ever measured weighed more than 2,000 pounds!

Plants on Coral Reefs

The Great Barrier Reef is home to more than 500 kinds of plants and algae. Many animals also eat the microscopic plankton that float in the water.

Seagrasses are an important part of the coral reef environment. They are true plants that have roots and flowers. Seagrasses are the main food for dugongs and sea turtles. Many small sea animals, such as prawns and fish, make their homes in the seagrasses. Seagrasses help keep the ocean water clean.

Seagrasses

Many kinds of algae live on coral reefs. Algae are not true plants. They lack roots and do not flower. They may be red, green, or brown. Plant-eating animals use algae for food. Seaweeds are large forms of algae. People use some kinds of seaweed in making ice cream, medicine, and makeup.

Sargassum, a brown algae

Dangers to Coral Reefs

Coral reefs face many dangers. Ten percent of the reefs in the world have already been destroyed. One danger is dynamite fishing. Fishermen explode dynamite near the reef to stun the fish so that they're easy to catch. At the same time, they damage the reef and kill other plants and animals. Some fishermen use poison to stun the fish. Poison also harms the reef and other living things.

Pollution is another danger to coral reefs. Pollution is adding harmful materials to the environment. Sewage and chemicals from the land often get into the ocean and damage the reefs. Sometimes large ships run into rocks and spill oil into the ocean. Oil kills many reef plants and animals.

Dynamite fishing

Another danger to coral reefs is **global warming**. Global warming is the gradual increase in the overall temperature of the air around Earth. Global warming causes ocean water to get warmer. The algae that live inside the coral polyps die from the warmer water. Without the food from the algae, the corals begin to starve. Then they turn white and die.

Tourists can be a danger to coral reefs. Sometimes they break off a piece of coral from the reef. Often they buy coral in a store. In both cases, the reef is damaged. People on boats sometimes throw their anchor into the shallow water and damage the reef. Also, people who wear sunscreen on their bodies and then swim in the ocean can poison the plants and animals on the reef.

Bleached coral

Building houses too close to the shore is also a danger to coral reefs. Mangrove trees and seagrasses grow on the land near coral reefs. These plants keep the soil on the land. People remove these plants before they build houses. Then the ocean waves wash the soil into the water onto the coral reefs. The soil blocks the sunlight that the corals need to live.

Mangrove trees

Protecting Coral Reefs

People can protect coral reefs that are healthy. They can help damaged reefs. One way to protect coral reefs is to create marine parks. No one may fish or hunt for coral in these parks. Over time, the fish return to these reefs, and the corals become healthy again.

Another way to protect coral reefs is to plant mangrove trees and other plants. The photo below shows a nursery that grows young mangrove plants. When these plants are bigger, they will help keep the soil on the land and protect the reefs.

Mangrove nursery

Another way to protect coral reefs is to reduce global warming. Air pollution is one cause of global warming. Using energy from the sun helps reduce air pollution. Some people put solar panels on their homes. These panels use the sun's energy to heat and light their houses. Solar panels can be used anywhere there is sun.

Doing reef checks is another way to help protect coral reefs. Some people know how to scuba dive. They work with groups that collect information about the health of coral reefs. They learn how to observe the reefs and report their observations.

Solar panels

How Can You Help?

Here are some things you can do to help protect coral reefs.

- Keep learning about coral reefs and the plants and animals that live on them.
- Support groups that protect coral reefs.
- Visit your local aquarium or zoo. Ask what they are doing and how you can help conserve our coral reefs.
- If you ever dive near a coral reef, don't touch anything.
- Don't throw trash on the ground. Recycle it to keep it out of the ocean.
- Conserve water. The less water you use, the less waste water gets into the ocean.
- Pick up litter and recycle it.
- Tell other people about the importance of coral reefs.

Now Try This

Build a Model of a Coral Polyp

Thousands of coral polyps build a coral reef. Building a model of a coral polyp will help you learn the body structure of this tiny animal. It will also help you review how plants and animals are different. In addition, it will help you understand how coral polyps and algae work together.

Single coral polyp

Materials – for each model

1 paper towel
1 paper plate
1 toothpick
1 plastic straw
1 section of banana (2" long)
6 candy straws or licorice sticks (cut into 1" pieces)
1 tsp. sugar sprinkles, the same color as candy straws
1 tsp. jam
1 round cracker
5–6 oyster crackers

1. Make a hole (the mouth) in the top half of the banana with a straw.

2. Make six holes with a toothpick surrounding the mouth.

3. Poke six candy straws (the tentacles) into the holes.

4. Add sprinkles (algae) to the banana.

5. Add round cracker and jam (coral attached to reef).

6. Add oyster crackers around the base (hard outer skeleton).

7. Place polyps together to form a colony model.

Glossary

algae *n.* very simple living things that grow in water

atoll *n.* a circular reef that goes around a lagoon

colony *n.* a group of animals living close together and forming a connected structure

coral *n.* a tiny, spineless animal with a tube-shaped body and a mouth surrounded by tentacles

coral polyp *n.* a tiny ocean animal that is about the size of your thumbnail

coral reef *n.* a ridge of hard rock formed by coral and found in warm, shallow ocean water

global warming *n.* the gradual increase in the overall temperature of the air around Earth

lagoon *n.* a body of salt water that is separated from the ocean

pollution *n.* the introduction of harmful substances into the environment

tentacle *n.* an armlike part of a sea animal used for catching food and for protection